From the Pit to the Pulpit

Molly Sexton Thomas

BK
ROYSTON
Publishing

BK Royston Publishing
P. O. Box 4321
Jeffersonville, IN 47131
502-802-5385
http://www.bkroystonpublishing.com
bkroystonpublishing@gmail.com

Cover Design: Brent Barnett
besquaredgraphicdesign@gmail.com

ISBN-13: 978-1-946111-64-7

Printed in the United States of America

Dedication

I dedicate this book to anyone who has experienced or currently going through abuse of any kind and never spoken about it. It is your time to be set free!

Acknowledgements

First, I like to thank God for always keeping me and blessing me throughout every aspect of my life.

To my children Latoya & Alisa Sexton for encouraging me & having patience with me through some of the most difficult times in my life. I love you.

Table of Contents

FROM THE PIT TO THE PULPIT

Chapter 1

While reading and meditating on the 23rd division of Psalms, it is so clear to me that when David wrote this passage he was looking back on his life. I can imagine him looking out of his window and thinking about how far God had brought him. From working as a shepherd boy to the reigning king, and all the trials and tribulations David went through, he arrives at the point of praising God despite it all. As I read this passage over and over, I see the deep sense of admiration and gratefulness David has toward God. I can just see David thinking about his life and retreating to a place of quietness, picking up a pen and paper, and writing the words of this 23rd Psalm, "The Lord is my Shepherd; I shall not want. He maketh me to lie down in green pasture; he leadeth me beside the still waters. He restoreth my soul; he leadeth me in the path of righteousness for his namesake. Yea, though I walk through the valley of the shadow of deaths, I will fear no evil; for thou art with me; thy rod and thy staff they comfort me. Thou preparest a table before me in the presence of mine enemies; thou anointest my head with oil; my cup runneth over. Surely goodness and mercy shall follow me all the days of my life, and I will dwell in the house of the Lord forever."

I have heard and recited those six verses many times, but I guess, like David, you have to go through some things to really appreciate the words. As I sit and meditate on my life, I began to feel David wrote those words just for me. I sit here now thanking God for all I have and where I came from. Now, let's get one thing straight, when I say things that I have, I am not talking about material items. They are good to have, but I am thanking God for my peace of mind, for my spirituality, my joy, for just blessing, and keeping me down through the years. As I look at my life now, I can't believe there was a time that I did not know if I believed in God or not.

Growing up, I lived in a small town in Indiana where there were no strangers, and everyone knew your name. The town had one high school that everyone attended. We had one K-Mart and two pharmacies. The railroad tracks divided the city. It was usually Northside versus Southside and each side had its own community center.

Northsiders gathered at Lakewood Community Center and Southsiders went to Crawford Community Center. Neighbors would sit on the porch in rocking chairs talking to each other and watch kids play stickball or four squares. Seems like each house was uniquely built for that specific family. No matter where we were in the town, you had better be home before the street lights came on. It seems like there was a church on every corner. I remember attending a beautiful white church that sits on the corner of Baxter Street. It was a small church with beautiful stain-glass windows and a white cross on top of the roof. The name of our church was Agape Baptist Church. It was a historical building because it was the oldest church in our community. Every Sunday it filled quickly so you would have to get there early to get

a seat. When you walked in the sanctuary, the first

thing you noticed was the drawing above the

baptismal pool. It was a picture of Jesus standing

in the clouds with his arms wide open and the

words "Come unto me, all ye that labor and are

heavy laden, and I will give you rest," Matthew

11:28. Beautiful white and black benches filled the

room and a black and white carpet divided them

and made an aisle. There was a black organ on one

side of the room and a black piano on the other

side. The choir stand was full every Sunday with

the youth choir on one side and the adult choir on

the other side. I was usually the little girl with her

hair in a pony tail sitting on the front seat of the

youth choir not really knowing what I was singing

about, but I was there singing mainly because my mother made me. Raised in a home where my mom was all about God and church, I was at the church every time the doors were open. But for some reason, it did not raise my interest in God. Now that I am older, and I look back on those days when I had to go to church, I guess something was happening inside of me that just took a long time to manifest.

I think about my childhood often. Sometimes I believed I was robbed of my childhood. My mother's name was Paula Mays. I don't have too many complaints of the childhood she gave me because now I realize she gave me the best that she could offer. Mom was a stern woman, who was not that loving, but I knew in her own way she loved me. She was not very affectionate. I can't even remember a hug or hearing her say, "I love you" except for a few days before she died. Even without her affection, I still knew that she loved me. I often wondered why she did not express her love by saying it or hugging me. Later in life, I found out Mom was that way because she lost her mother at a young age and she did not receive a lot of affection. I lived in a home with my Mom, Dad and a brother, Jack, who was a teenager when I was born. Jack was a good brother most of the time, but you know how sibling rivalry goes; I believe he was jealous of me many times. Other than that, I feel like he was a good brother most of the time. On the outside looking in, you would think I had the best childhood. When you grow up with secrets and lies, it is nothing but a recipe for disaster. That's how my childhood was, secrets and lies.

Chapter 2

Back in those days, when grown-ups would get together, children would have to disappear. You had better not be caught trying to stay in a room when grown folks were talking, because that is when secrets were being discussed. I learned that I lived in a house full of secrets and lies. When those secrets started to come out, my life turned upside down forever. There are so many things that happened in my life, I don't even know where to start. I guess I could start with the one with my dad. I know I said my mother was not very affectionate, but my dad was. I remember my dad kissing me and touching me from as far back as when I was five years old. I never did understand why it was a secret. He always told me

9

you are my special girl and you can't tell anybody what we do. He would buy me anything I wanted. I did not know what he was doing was wrong. I remember when I was young, he would sit me on an ironing board. I don't like iron boards to this day, because I was molested on an ironing board. The ironing board is a place to straighten out wrinkles, but my life became more complicated and wrinkled at the ironing board.

My Dad was always feeling on me, touching me and saying I was special, and gave me anything I wanted after he took me off the ironing board. As I think about this now, I feel so dirty and ashamed. To be honest, I thought that is what dads did. However, looking back on it I feel like I was a little prostitute. It is sad to say, but the ironing board experience is all I can remember about my dad because he was either playing with my chest or sticking his hands in my pants. Sometimes I remember his touch would hurt so badly down there, and I would say, "That hurts."

His reply would be, "it is supposed to, but it will stop. It's just our special secret and I am preparing you for life, you are my special girl."

Hey, I was young, and I believed him. So, Dad continued to put his hands in my pants. I was being molested and I did not even know it. All I knew was if I let my Dad put his hands in my pants, I got anything I wanted. I am so embarrassed about this now.

This went on for years. I was in elementary school and Dad was still molesting me. However, he told me if I told anyone they would not believe me and that I would be put in a home where I wouldn't see my Mom anymore. Or, I would not be able to have nice things anymore. He even went on to say if I told, it would hurt my mother because she would think I was a liar. I loved my Mom and never wanted to hurt her. I do know the older I got, the more uncomfortable it made me. I remember I was in 4th grade, and I was going to Trayson Elementary School and they had a sex education class that your parents had to give permission for us to attend. My mom signed the permission slip, and I was able to attend the class. It was two separate classes one for girls and one for boys. In the girls' class, we learned about our menstrual cycle and how to keep ourselves clean. Then we were taught about touches to our bodies and what were good touches and bad touches. I was so shocked when I found out that what my dad was doing to me was a bad touch. I could not belicve this nurse was telling me that if someone touches you down there it was a bad touch. A man was not supposed to touch little girls in that manner and if someone did, we should tell our parents. Just imagine how confused I was, because my parent was the one who was touching me down there. I thought my dad said I was special? I was not supposed to tell anyone because it was our secret. Then I thought this teacher did not know what she was talking about, I'm telling my Dad what she said. People might not believe this, but I thought about this the whole day. I remember when I got home from school, I could not wait until my Dad came home. I continued looking out the window, so I could run outside and tell him what that teacher said. I just knew he was going to be mad and probably go to the school and tell that teacher off.

He finally pulled up, and I can remember this just as if it was yesterday. I ran outside, and I said, "I got something to tell you."

He said, "What is it?"

I said, "My teacher said that if you touch me down there it is wrong, and no one is supposed to touch me down there."

I got a reaction, but not the one I thought. I was thinking he was going to be mad at the teacher or nurse, but instead, he got mad at me.

He grabbed me by my arm and said, "Did you tell them anything?"

I said, "No."

He said, "You better not tell them nothing, because if you do they are not going to believe you and put you in jail or take you away and put you in a home and we will never see you again. If they do that, you won't have a bike or new clothes or anything. You won't see your mom anymore, and you will hurt her. Is that what you want?"

By this time, I am crying. I said, "No."

He said, "You better not say anything, especially to your Mom or anybody at school."

That's when I learned what was being done to me was wrong. I was being molested and the weird thing about it is after I told him all that, he kept doing it; not as often, but it was being done. I was scared to say anything. I feared the man I called Dad. Everyone else loved him, especially my Mom. I think that is when I began to lose something inside of me like my self-worth. I began to feel dirty. I started taking so many baths, trying to wash away the feeling of being ashamed. There was a hurt in the inside of me and I'm trying to wash it off, but it is not going nowhere. When innocence has been taken from you it gives you a dirty feeling. No matter how many baths you take, only God can wash you clean. I believe that is when I first started not liking who I was. I did not like anything about me, my hair or my body. I felt ugly and when I looked in the mirror all I saw was an ugly person. I started my life of pretending.

When I say pretending, I mean acting like nothing was wrong. A smile was on my face but hurt and emptiness was in my heart. I would try everything I could not to be alone with my Dad, but sometimes it was unavoidable. I remember one time we lived on 12th Street above a barbeque business. On the weekends, they would have dances. I would always have to be in the house at a certain time.

My Mom would say, "You need to stay in because those men could do bad things to you."

I would think to myself, it couldn't be any worse than what my Dad is doing, but I kept my mouth shut. I thought I was the only one my Dad was touching, I found out differently. While living on Baker Street, I became friends with a young girl in a family across the street and another girl who lived beside us. We all would get together and play and stay the night at each other's house. They were my best friends. One day I was playing with the girl across the street, and we got into an argument as kids do.

Suddenly, she said, "And I am not staying at your house anymore." I asked why? She told me because my Dad was always trying to give her money, so he could feel on her. Of course, I was in shock!

I said, "No he doesn't!"

My other little friend said, "Yes he does."

Then one of them said, "I am telling my mom."

The next thing I know, they left and went home. A few hours later, it was all over the block that my Dad was molesting people. Some people were going to my Dad's defense, and some believed it.

All I remember is my Mom crying and saying to me, "I know he did not do this. We must stick together. Now the police are going to come over here, and you need to tell them that John did not do anything to you. If you say he did, they might take you away from me."

I believe in my heart she knew what he was doing. He took good care of us financially. I don't blame my mom for what happened.

She went on to say, "So if they talk to you, then you better tell them no."

My mom was crying so I told her okay. A few hours later, the police came. They talked to my mom first.

I heard her say, "I asked her, and she said he has never touched her, but you can ask her."

My mom called me into the kitchen all I could see was this police officer, his gun, and me being taken away from my mom. I could feel her staring at me.

He asked my mom to leave the room then he said, "I am going to ask you a question, and I want you to tell me the truth. Has your dad every touched you in the wrong way?"

The only thing I could think about is they are going to take me away from my mom. They are going to put me in jail and I don't want to hurt my mom.

So, I said, "No, he has not."

The police officer said, "ok." and he left.

I believe that was the biggest mistake of my life. Why didn't I tell the truth; why didn't I say no?

Chapter 3

We moved from Baker Street. We never heard anything else about that incident with the police. Of course, the streets were talking some about my dad. Some people defended my dad and said he would never do anything like that, while others said yes, "he did do it."

Years later, I learned that some of the parents did not take it any further because they did like my mom. My friends later said Dad had never really touched them, he was just asking them to let him. I don't know, but I know my life changed. From that time on, I was teased about my dad messing with me. Seems like I was always trying to defend myself. I think this is the start of my anger festering down inside. I was denying something that was true, but I did not know what else to do at the time. People can have their thoughts about what they would have done at the time, but until you are in that situation at a young age, you don't know what you would do. Some people had the nerve to say that I liked being molested, that's why I did not say anything. I was a child. I did not know what to do but keep a secret and make my mom happy. About this time, I was 10 or 11 and Mom trusted me to be with some of my school friends at the Lakewood Community Center. This was a place in our community where we would go to play and hang out with friends. Mr. Thompson operated the community center, he was such a great man, always had things for us to do at the center. It was at the center that I had my second life changing event. People always came to the center to meet with Mr. Thompson. I remember a woman was talking to him one day and she came over to where we were playing four squares. I can't remember her name, but she was talking to some of us.

She said to me, "You look just like your mother."

I said, "How do you know my mom?"

She replied, "I know your mother, Janice."

"I was like, huh? My mother's name is not Janice my mom's name is Paula Mays"

She looked at me crazy and said, "I thought your mother's name was Janice."

I said, "no" and kept on playing.

The funny thing was being that I knew a woman named Janice, but she was not my mother. She was my mother's friend and she had a son who my mom kept. His name was Michael, but we called him "Mo."

He used to live with us, but for some reason, Janice came and took him one day. So, I knew who the lady was talking about, but how could she think she was my mother. I was kind of flattered that she thought Janice was my mother. Even though I did not see Janice a lot, when I did see her, I thought she was the most beautiful woman ever. When Janice came to our house, I would just like to look at her because she was always dressed so nice, her hair was stylish, and she always smelled good. Many times, when she came over, I remember she would bring me a doll or something. She was my Mom's friend who brought gifts. Hey, I wished all her friends who came to visit had gifts. She did not come often, but when she did, there was a gift. When it was time to leave the center, and I was walking home and thought about what the woman said. How could she think Janice was my mother? I looked nothing like her. When I got home, I told my Mom about the lady at the center who said I looked like Janice. I thought my mother was going to find it as funny as I did, but nope. She was very angry with me and asked who the nosey woman was. I told her I did not know who she was. My mom was so mad and said I was not going back to the center for a while. She told me she was my mother and not to listen to anyone else. I could not believe she got so mad at me. I knew she was my Mom, but why was she yelling at me and forbidding me to go to the center. Wow, all of this because I told her what someone else had said. I needed to learn to keep my mouth shut. My mom had a sister who was my favorite person, Aunt Dee. She was the best lady in the world to me. She and her husband were like my second parents. Aunt Dee was awesome. If there was a perfect woman, it was my Aunt Dee.

Mom and Aunt Dee were close sisters and they would talk on the phone 2 or 3 times a day or visit each other every day. They would go shopping together or the laundry mat. They were as close as any sisters could be. I often wished I had a sister to be close with like they were. I remember hearing my Mom tell my Aunt what I told her about the woman saying I look like Janice. I could not fully understand everything they were saying, but I do remember Aunt Dee saying, "you are going to have to tell her one day."

When I heard that, it just stuck in my head. It is amazing how certain things will stick with you. As time went on, and I got older, more and more people told me I look like Janice or she was my mother. Then I started to look at our family dynamics. Mom was brown skinned, Dad was darker than she was, and my brother, Jack, had dark skin, but I was light skinned. I wondered why I was light skinned and they are not. Once again, I foolishly told my Mom that someone said Janice was my mother. Once again, she was very mad, just went off and told me I needed to stop coming to her with that nonsense. Furthermore, if I came to her again with that mess I was not going to go anywhere. Once again, I felt like I had done something wrong. This is the time I started just shutting down, and not saying anything to my mom. I decided not to say anything to my Dad because there was not trust or communication with him. After I found out molestation was wrong, our relationship became non-existent. I could not talk to Jack because he was grown and married. Because of the molestation, I had begun to shut down on the inside anyway. Now the mention of Janice being my mother caused me to get in trouble. I really did not say much but I thought about it a lot. When Janice would come to visit, I would just stare at her and wish she were my mother. She was beautiful. I would have thought, 'if Janice was my mother, I could tell her things and she would not get mad. She wouldn't tell me to lie to the police. I would be beautiful like she was, smell good like she does and dress like she does. I wish she was my mother.' I love my mom, but it was just something about Janice. Every time I saw her I was in awe.

Now Janice had two children; Trice and of course Mo who I mentioned earlier. They were the only ones I knew about at the time. Mo used to live with us and Trice lived with Janice's mother, Ms. Betty, who was my Mom's friend. They would visit each other a lot. Either Ms. Betty would come over to our house or we would visit her. That is how I got to know Trice. However, I noticed after I told Mom people were saying Janice was my mother, we didn't visit Ms. Betty as much. I did not understand why, but I would soon to find out. As I grew older, people would tell me I looked like Janice. I could not understand why people would say that. I knew I could not ask Mom because she would get mad and I would end up in trouble. I just kept thinking Mom said these people were lying, she did not know why they would tell me Janice was my mom they just wanted to start trouble and be nosey. I was going to believe my mom. She would not lie to me because moms did not lie to their children. She believed in God church and always told me He did not like people who lied. She would always stress how important it was for me to tell the truth. I remember one time I did something wrong my mom questioned me about it, and I told her a lie. She found out that I lied. I got my butt whooped, a lecture on how God hates liars, hell is where liars ended up and people did not trust liars.

So, if my mom said Janice is not my mother, then it is what it is, she is not my mother. I could not understand why other people were saying different, but my mom said it was a lie and I believed my mother, point, blank, period. So, I just tried to ignore what others were saying, but I heard it a lot. I remember one day I was walking home from the center with a bunch of kids, I can't remember what we were doing, but Janice was in a car that pulled up beside me.

She looked at me and said, "You better get home, it is getting dark."

Ok, me being a kid and with some other children I looked at her and said, "You don't tell me what to do!" to which she replied, "Girl I will beat your butt!"

I said, "No you won't, I will tell my Mom on you too."

The next thing that came out of her mouth was just awful. She looked at me and said, "I am your mother."

I was just floored. Why would she tell me that? I said, "No you're not and leave me alone!"

One of my friends who was with me said, "I did not know she was your mother."

I looked at her and said Janice was not my mother she is my mom's friend. About this time, we caught up with Trice and some of his friends. Trice asked me if I told his momma she was not my mother. I guess Janice saw him and told him what I said. I confirmed what I said to Janice, because I was tired of hearing it. Trice told me she was my mother, and he was my brother. Talk about stunned. We argued back and forth on the matter, but that did not stop Trice. He said my Mom was not telling me the truth.

I said no because I asked my mom, and she said she was my mom, so you just stop lying. He replied look sis I am not lying to you Aunt Paula is the one lying. I could not believe this boy is telling me that my mom is lying,

I was so confused. I knew that I could not go home and say anything to my mom. I would be in trouble. What was I going to do? Who is my mom? Do I have brothers besides Jack? What is going on? I was 13 years old and overwhelmed with thoughts about Janice being my mother. I didn't live with her, and she was not taking care of me. If Janice was my mother, then the man I called Dad was not my father. Was that the reason he did those bad things to me? I was totally lost and did not know who I was, or who my parents were. Did my mom look me in the face and do what she always tells me not to do and that was lie? I am so confused at this point, I don't know who to talk too. I have been abused by my dad, and I don't know who my mother is. Now I got all these people telling me I look like a woman that I can't even mention to my mom. Life was just so confusing for me at the age of 13.

I went to my Aunt Dee's house for answers, besides my mom she was the other person I trusted. I sat there wondering how to bring all this up to her. She and my Mom were close, and I did not want her to say anything to my mom. After being there for a while, I finally had the courage to say something to her. I told her what Trice said and how mad I was about it, especially because he called my mom a liar.

My Aunt looked at me and said, "I am going to tell you the truth. Janice is your birth mother, but Paula is your mother also." Now I was confused! How could they both be my mother, and what was a birth mother?

Then Aunt Dee told me, "Paula is your mother because she is raising you as her child. You were not born to her, but she is taking care of you. Janice gave birth to you, but she could not take care of you, so Paula wanted you. She and John chose to raise you as their own."

Aunt Dee went on to say Paula loves you, she just did not know how to tell you the truth. I feel like you deserve to know the truth, just don't say nothing to Paula right now. At this time, I did not hear the part about how much my Mom loved me, all I heard was that she is not my mother, and she lied. Janice was my mother and did not want me. I was hurt and mad at everyone except Aunt

38

Dee because she did tell me the truth. I knew we had a special bond. I also knew if I let Mom know Aunt Dee told me the truth, the bond they had would be ruined. So, I never told her. I was very upset, how could this be, no wonder my dad was molesting me, I was not his. Jack was not my real brother; my whole life was a lie.

Chapter 4

My mother had a best friend named Ellen. I always called her Auntie E. She had children and we referred to each other as cousins. However, for some strange reason, I called her husband Mr. Allen. I see him one day and I said hi Mr. Allen. His respond was girl stop calling me Mr. Allen, I am your Uncle. I laughed and said oh yes because I say Auntie E, he responded that was not the reason he was my real uncle. I was like, huh? Uncle Allen told me Janice was my mother and his sister. Now, this was another shock for me because I did not know Janice was his sister. Furthermore, here is another person telling me that Janice is my mother. For some reason, I had doubted when everyone else told me this, but I knew that Aunt

Dee and Mr. Allen were telling me the truth. He was always a stand-up man who looked out for me. He made sure I was ok when he saw me on the streets. I thought it was because his wife and my mother were good friends. I just knew what he was telling me was the truth. He said exactly what Aunt Dee told me. Now it made sense. Trice told me the truth. He was my brother; now who are my sisters. As a matter of fact, who was my Dad?

After hearing all that news, my childish mind tried to bring clarity to the whole situation. I started to question whether God was real or doubt who God was because my mom drug me to church every Sunday and told me to always tell the truth, yet she was holding on to the biggest lie ever. It was no wonder to me that the man I though was my dad molested me because I was not really his child; consequently, he did not care about me. As my life continued to spiral out of control, I reasoned that Janice didn't care about me or she would have kept me. Then I thought that evidently God didn't care about me because He let me go through all of it. I thought I had not done anything wrong to deserve their treatment. I was so confused because for my mother to give me away, for my dad to do all these bad things to me, for my mom has lied to me and I don't know who my dad is, wow this is a lot. I can't say anything to my mom she has already made it clear that she does not want to hear anything about Janice being my mother. As I review this new information, to me, it was just getting worse. For years, I felt alone and wanted sisters and brothers only to find out I do have them, and they are Janice's children. The sad part was that none of them lived with Janice either. She had given all of her children to someone else to raise. It was hard trying to get to know my brothers and sisters while pretending that I did not know anything about them. I had to act like I did not know nothing about Janice being my mother around my mom. I had to act like Jack was my only brother. I had other brothers and sisters that I could not acknowledge. I think this is the time when rebellion set in. I did not want to go to church, but I had to go. At this point, I really did not want to hear anything about God. Plus, other things started happening to me. One day when I was 14, my Mom and Dad had not gotten home

44

from work yet and I was home alone. My Mom's cousin, Billyboy is what we called him, came over and I let him in because he had been over many times before so consequently, I did not give it a second thought. When I opened the door, I told him my Mom was not home yet. He said he would just wait and asked what I was doing, to which I replied homework. He had been sitting for a moment when suddenly, the next thing I know he grabs my breasts and was trying to pull my pants down. I started trying to fight him, but he was too big. I could not defend myself. The struggle continued as he pulled my pants down and was trying to enter me. Then he started putting his mouth on my breasts and all I could do was cry. He told me if I ever told anybody, he would kill me. I did believe him and I feared him. From that point on, I believe I started hating myself. I never told Mom, but I was always terribly afraid when he came around. He would look at me in a way that sent shivering chills throughout my body. Later, I found out that I was not the only person Billybob had molested. I had a best friend Kate and one day when we were grown, we were talking about our childhood and things that had happened. I told her about Billybob and she said he did the same thing to her.

After that incident, I just did not want to be around anyone. I became very introverted. However, I found a love for basketball which gave me an escape from my life. In the meantime, I found out more about my brothers and sisters. My sister, Sidney, lived about three blocks from me. Members of her father's family raised her and they were very open. They told her who her mother was, and she knew all her brothers and sisters. As we grew older, she told me a story of when we were in school. She told someone I was her sister and how I replied that I was not her sister. She said that I had really hurt her feelings. I explained to her, I really did not know she was my sister at the time that I denied her. Anyway, when I found out she was my sister, I had to sneak to play with her. I would tell Mom I was going to the Community Center, but instead, I would go over to her house and play. My mother just did not want me to have anything to do with my siblings. I came from a small town where everyone knew each other, so how could I ignore them? I made my mom think I did not know them which made her happy while I was miserable. By this time, she knew that I had found out the truth. I had to act like I didn't like my siblings or Janice.

All I know is, I had a very unhappy childhood. I was supposed to go to church and act as if I loved this great God everyone was talking about. I had a Mom that did not want me. It appears every time I turned around, someone was molesting me. The person who I thought was my mother lied to me and did not want me to acknowledge my real family. I still didn't know who was my father? So, to me, I did not think God was so great and that He did not love me. On top of everything, I learned more about Janice and that everyone knew about my life except me. People at church knew that Paula was not my real mother. They would talk about how great she was and how awesome my dad was, but by this time, they were raising more kids, and my brother Jack was beginning to have kids. Now, I spent my life making sure my dad did not do the same things to those girls that he had done to me.

I love my mom, but it was so hard living in that house, always watching and make sure my foster sisters or my nieces were not being molested. Pretending that I was happy when I was not. I was living in a house of lies and secrets. I always tell people now that I lived in a house, not a home. I spent my teenage years wondering who I was, not being happy.

Even with my Aunt Dee, I could not tell her what Dad had done to me or what happened to me with their cousin, Billybob. I began to feel as though I was not important. Since my brother began to have children, Mom was focused on her grandchildren. The little attention she showed me now went to her grandchildren. I never took my frustrations out on them, but in a way, I resented them. I just felt like a lost child that no one wanted or loved. I was becoming bitter inside. I loved Mom, but I did not like her. She lied to me. If you can't trust your mom then who can you trust? It seems like everyone that smiled in my face was lying to me.

I just could not understand how a loving God, who cared so much about people could let these things happen to me. I tried to do everything right. I got good grades in school, tried not to tell lies, and did not steal. I tried to love people but did not feel their love in return. The more I found out about my brothers and sisters, the more I wanted to be with them, but I couldn't. My mom did not want me to have anything to do with them and that hurt. In fact, she stopped hanging around Ms. Betty, because she did not want me to be around Trice. I figured out they were my grandparents, but I could not acknowledge them around Mom.

Chapter 5

As I grew older and was able to go anywhere I wanted, I hung around my brothers and sisters. As I got to know my cousins, I had a great time, but when I got home, I lied about where I had been or who I was with. This was sad for a teenager. I should be able to love freely and bond with my biological family. I still had to go and remain active at church, which was the last place I wanted to be. I was on the usher board and sung in the choir. I did not mind the usher board but singing about a God who was supposed to love everyone was not what I felt like doing. At that time, I could care less about God. My thoughts were that He did not care about me, so why should I care about Him. However, the church was a part of my life whether I liked it or not. So, I pretended that I loved the church because that made Mom happy. I discovered that if she was happy I could go anywhere I wanted, which meant I could hang out with my family.

Just when you think things are ok, and you are trying to adjust to the hand that life has dealt you, something else happens. I was about 15 at the time when Mom would have friends drop over for a visit from time to time. I was not feeling well one day when one of my mom's friends and her husband came to visit. Mom told them I was sick, and she was not going to send me to school and I would be home by myself until she had got off work. Mom was a cook at a children's home, so she did not work many hours. Her friend told her she would check on me. Mom thought that was a great idea. So, the next morning I stayed home, and she went to work. About an hour after Mom left, there was a knock at the door. In those days, people were very trusting and usually did not look to see who was at the door before opening it. I figured it was Mom's friend checking on me. Instead, it was her friend's husband. I opened the door before noticing it was him and he quickly came in, shut the door, and begin to grab on me. I told him my Mom would be home soon, but it did not stop him. He threw me on the couch and raped me. I could not believe this was happening to me. When he was done, he made me feel like it was my fault. I felt so ashamed and hurt. He talked to me as if I was nothing. He told me I better not say nothing or he was going to kill me. He said nobody would believe me. He called me a bitch and said I was nothing just like my real mother. No one would believe he raped me, because I was not worth raping. So, I better keep my mouth shut. Now, I had heard rumors that he had been caught peeping in people's windows. I never thought he would rape someone, especially me because we were like family!

The bad part about it, I believed every word he said. I really started hating myself. I felt like I was nothing. On top of that, I began to hear stories about Janice. I also found out how people in our small town felt about her. They called her names and said she was a whore who did not know how to do anything, but have babies and give them up.

People would say her kids were nothing because nothing from nothing leaves nothing. For years, I had admired Janice. I thought she was smart, beautiful, and someone who always brought me a toy when she came to visit Mom. Now I saw her in a different light. She had a bad reputation in our city. I thought that it caused people to use and abuse me because of her. This is where my distain for her started. She was no longer beautiful to me. She was a person who had caused me a lot of hurt and pain. It was like I had a love and hate feeling toward her all at the same time. After I found out Janice was my mother, she did not treat me the same as she did before. I remember seeing her on the streets and she would turn her head or just over look me altogether. If it was not true, that is how I felt.

Since I lived in a small town, my brothers and I had mainly the same friends. We were all hanging out at the schoolyard one day when Janice drove up in a car. She said hello to everyone and gave my two brothers $10 each. When she looked at me, she said, "I will get you later." That really hurt my feelings. Then my oldest brother, Trice, gave me $5 of his money. I did not take it from him because I had some money, but that was not the point. Janice had no problem telling me she was my mother, but she had a problem acting like my mother. I really believed that Janice did not like me. She must have hated me because she did give me away. I used to think she gave me away because I was ugly.

It is sad to realize you have led an unhappy life because of others. There was no one I really felt like I could talk to about what I had been through and that was depressing. There was a time when I felt like killing myself. I used to dream about jumping off a bridge or shooting myself. I remember one time I did go to the bridge to jump but when I got there, I just could not go through with it. I guess that was God working behind the scenes and I did not realize it. I also looked for a gun but could not find one. Just my misfortune, I thought. Every time I thought about the molestations and rapes, I wanted to kill myself. I would do things just to hurt myself. One time, I broke my own arm. I kept hitting my arm with a rock until I broke it. What's worse, I did not really feel any pain while I did it. Another time I cut myself with a knife while I was washing dishes. I started thinking about things, and then I cut my hand with a knife--not my wrist, but my hand. I had 14 stitches and a sore hand because of stupidity. That was not the end. Later in my life, I made more stupid mistakes because pain was all I knew. I inflicted the pain on my own self. The devil really had me then.

All those times I went through my trials at a young age and did not want to acknowledge God, I now see God was working behind the scenes. I was mad at God, but He was setting me up for something I could never imagine. I can't really say I was a happy person because I wasn't. I just survived to please everyone else. I lost myself a long time ago and did not know how to find me. I strived to make Mom happy, my nieces, and nephews happy. Singer Smokey Robinson had a song entitled, "Tears of a Clown." One of the verses of the lyrics reads, "If there's a smile on my face, it's only there trying to fool the public." That is how I felt. I did not know how to be happy except to do everything everyone else wanted me to do. Now I know why I have such a passion for people who are hurting, especially children separated from their parents. I hate to see a sad child; it reminds me so much of my childhood. Whenever I see someone who looks sad or unhappy, I always try to talk to them and let them know they are special. Now that I have children, I try every way possible to make them happy and let them know how special they are to me. I never really thought I was able to truly love unconditionally until I had my first daughter. When I saw her, all I could feel was love. I knew she would love me no matter what I looked like or what size I was; she was my baby.

I vowed the day she was born that I would never let anyone hurt her and I would do all I could to make her feel wanted and happy. While I was growing up, I always said I did not want any children because of the rape and the molestation. I did not want anything that had to do with sex. Until one day, I met a guy at my sister's house. He was not my first boyfriend, but he was the first one

I had feelings for. At first, he seemed so sweet and gave me lots of attention. He told me I was special, cute, and all the things I never heard. I thought I was in love with him, so I made the mistake of moving in with him. The only good thing that came out of the relationship was my daughter. Jason was fine at first. I thought that maybe I would be happy with him forever. But that turned out to be a bust! He became verbally abusive by calling me out of my name, but then he would buy me something to make up. One day he got mad at something that happened outside of our home. He came home and thought he was going to take his frustrations out on me. Arguing was one thing, but then for no reason he slapped me and punched me in the face. Then he told me I was no better than my mother was. He said I was a tramp just like her. I got up and pushed him then hit him back. He hit me again. I knew where his gun was, and I was determined not to let another man violate me in any kind of way again. So, I went in the bedroom, got his gun, walked in the living room, and pointed at him. He tried to be brave and told me to shoot, but I could see the fear in his eyes. I was slowly starting to pull the trigger and then my baby started to cry. I came to my senses when I heard her. Our daughter was the reason I did not kill him. I just told him to get out of my house. He left, and we were never together again. When I look back, I say my daughter saved her daddy's life and kept me from going to jail. I think because of the molestations, rape, and an abusive relationship, I really did not trust men anymore. I had a few relationships after that but nothing serious. I just could not relate to men when it came to the bedroom. I just really could not get into sex. Every time I would have sexual relations my mind would reflect to the rape or molestation. I just could not get into sex. So that caused a lot of problems in my relationships.

Sometimes with a few guys I dated, when we got to the point of sex, I would break up with them. I never have enjoyed sex, and that's why I was shocked when I got pregnant with my youngest daughter. Her dad was a good man, but we always had a debate about sex. He felt like I was not engaging, when it came to that part of our relationship. The old saying is true "if you don't meet your man's needs at home, he will go and find someone who will." That is exactly what he did. The next thing I knew he was messing with another woman and both of us were pregnant at the same time. Here I am with two kids and no daddy. That was fine because I wasn't being pressured for sex all the time. I was determined to make sure my kids had a good life with or without a father. I was not going to keep any secrets from them. I wanted my girls to have the best and I wanted to be the best for them.

Chapter 6

As they grew up and I grew older, I knew there was something missing from my life. It was not because of my parents or some of the abuse I had gone through. It was something deep down that I just could not explain. I really was not satisfied. I think I was restless and kept searching for something I could not explain. I felt like I was searching for happiness, but I could not obtain it. So, I did things to try to achieve happiness. I started partying a lot and going out every weekend. I always made sure my kids were cared for, then I would hit the party scene. But, I just could not get into it like everyone else. I did not drink or get high, but I just like being in the place dancing and having fun with my friends. One day I was at a bar with my sister, an older gentleman sat next to me and started talking. He asked me a question. Not really wanting to be bothered, I allowed him to do so. He looked at me and said, "What are you doing in this place? You don't belong here."

I was kind of shocked! I really did not know what to say. The look on his face was so stern and sincere. It was the kind of question that you usually give a smart reply to the person. However, his words hit my heart for some reason.

I looked at him and said, "I don't know."

I looked away and when I turned back around to him, he was gone. That kind of bothered me all that night. I was still going to church, but the church was not in me. I was going to church out of habit; it was what I was raised to do, and I did it. I did not feel right staying home or keeping my girls home because they loved the church. It still had not hit me how good God was. I was working through the week, partying on Friday and Saturday, then going to church on Sunday. I was acting like some of the people I had heard my mother talk about and she would call them a hypocrite. I was a hypocrite I was acting like I loved God, but I really did not feel that way in my heart. I was still carrying a lot of hurt and pain. I thought the emptiness that I felt inside was from the molestation, rape, and feeling abandoned because of not having my biological parents in my life.

I had two wonderful girls who loved me unconditional. So why did I still feel alone and empty inside? I worked a good job in a factory where I was a team leader, so I made good money, but something was still missing out of my life and I did not know what it was. One day on the job, I went off because people were messing up products. Another co-worker and I were talking and cussing. I happened to look over at a new hire and her facial expression reminded me of the man in the bar. Every time I would cuss, I looked over at her, and her facial expressions did something to my heart. I decided I was going to talk to her to see what she was about. Rhonda was her name and her husband was a minister. I thought, 'oh no another religious freak.' I was raised to respect people, so I told the other co-worker to cool it on the cussing out of respect. As the weeks went by, I got close to Rhonda. Then, she did the unthinkable and invited me to a Bible study at her house. She kept asking me to come. I told her I would, but I really did not want to go. She had invited another lady also. She was excited to go. I was not, yet I reluctantly agreed to go. The night of the Bible study, my girls went skating with their cousins. I decided I was going to stay home and not go to the Bible study. I tried to do everything I could not to go, but I became restless. It seemed like time was passing by slowly. I went over to my Aunt Dee's house and I told her I was supposed to go to a Bible study but changed my mind. One thing about Aunt Dee, she would say things to make you think.

She asked me, "if you gave your word to Rhonda then you should be there right?" She followed that question with a... hmmm. I knew by her response I needed to get to that Bible study, so I got in my car and went to bible study.

I think after I attended that Bible study, it put me on the path that I am on now. Their Bible study was so powerful, it opened my eyes to look at God in a different way. They were talking about the love of God. At first, I thought, oh no I don't want to talk about God's love because I did not feel His love. I still had hurt and pain inside of me. I sure did not feel any love. I did not even want to love God. As I kept going to the Bible study, I began to start feeling something different in my heart. Maybe I should try to get to know God. One day at the Bible study a lady got up and started talking about the things she had been through, how it made her bitter and she hated the world. She stated how she did not trust anyone because of what she had been through. Every word she said hit me in my heart, because I felt her pain. I hated people and myself, the only good thing I had going for me was my girls. The lady just kept on talking, then she said, but through Jesus, she could love despite what she had been through. She said she had to learn how to forgive and learn how to be happy.

She kept saying, "Forgiveness is the key, forgiveness is the key. I don't know who I am talking to, but you got to forgive so you can live." That statement kept going through my mind, "you got to forgive to live." After I got home, I got to thinking about living. I had two daughters I needed to live for. I did not want unforgiveness to consume my life so much that I would not be able to live for my girls.

I kept going to bible study. I was invited to visit the church that Rhonda attended. I was used to going to church so that was not a problem for me. But since I had been going to Bible study, I understood I needed to have a different attitude about church. I went to Bible study for answers about why God let me go through some of the things that I had gone through and was still going through. I never did get those answers, but the Bible studies gave me a desire to learn more about God. So, when I got the invitation to visit their church, I decided to attend. The first time I went, I was a little nervous. I was going in with a new expectation. I was searching for something. What I did not know at the time, but there was a burning desire inside me. I needed to know what it was and how do I get rid of it. So just maybe I could get the answer at church. The Pastor was a tall man who had a stern tone to his voice. When he preached it was in such a way that really captured your attention. I will never forget his sermon was entitled, "Forgiveness will set you Free." He took his text from Matthew 6:14, "For if you forgive men their trespasses, your heavenly Father will also forgive you." I understood what he was talking about, but I really needed to understand the word 'trespass.' I found out that it meant an unlawful act causing injury to a person or property, committed with force or violence, actual or implied. The Pastor kept preaching about how you must forgive to heal. If you did not heal it was hindering your blessing and keeping you from enjoying what life has to offer.

Then the Pastor said, "Somebody here has been holding on to hurt. Somebody here wants to be set free and just don't know what to do. Somebody here is tired of hurting, feeling lonely, and sad. Well, there is a way out. Jesus has you here for a reason. You did not visit this church by accident this meeting was ordained by God. You are waiting on God, but God is waiting for you. Come take this chair not because I say so, but because God said it is time to give it all to him."

I was sitting there listening and something just came over me. I kept thinking, I did not come here for this. I am not ready. However, the more I sat there, the stronger the feeling was for me to go sit in that seat. But I just could not do it. I felt like the pastor was talking to me and everyone was staring at me. It was like in the cartoons where there is an angel on one shoulder and a devil on the other. The angel was saying go sit in the seat and the devil was saying it's a trick stay seated. I listened to the devil that day, I did not move. After church was over, a woman whom I had known for a while came up to me and said, "Honey the Spirit was talking to you."

I just looked at her and left thinking I was not coming back to this church. I did not go to the home Bible study that week, but I was troubled in my spirit. I could not eat or sleep that whole week.

I thought about the sermon on forgiveness. I thought about what the preacher was saying about being happy and you must forgive to heal. I questioned why I should forgive people who hurt me, lied to me and abandoned me. I didn't know how to forgive or where to start. I decided I was not going to anyone and tell them I forgave them. How do you forgive people, especially ones that have molested, raped, lied and abandoned you? But I wanted to be happy. I wanted to live. I wanted to be able to take care of my kids. I wanted them to be happy and proud of me as their mom. I didn't want to hurt anymore. I was tired of being depressed and mad all the time. I remembered thinking about all of this as I sat in my living room chair as tears streamed down my cheeks.

I remember saying, "God if you are real, please help me. If You love me like You say in Your word, please help. I can't do this anymore. I want to love my children the right way and I don't want to hurt anymore. I want to be loved. I wanted to be accepted. I need Your help. I am tired. I learned that the first step to healing is realizing that you need help."

I needed help! After going through that little transition, I decided to go back to church. I went in and sat down. The choir was singing and it sounded wonderful. Then, it was time for the sermon. The pastor started preaching about Mephibosheth from 2 Samuel chapter 9. He explained that Mephibosheth was the son of Johnathan who had been accidently injured by his handmaiden. The title was, "Crippled by Someone Else's Hand." He talked about how we can be hurt by other people and they can cripple us physically and mentally. But, if we trust in God, He still will show us favor. He went on to say that things we go through are not designed to break us, but to make us. It seemed like the pastor was talking to me again. He went on to say, "God allows us to go through because He knows we can handle it. You become strong through the things that you suffer." Then he said, "through your test becomes a testimony."

Through those words I finally began to feel God. I recall the sermon on the story of Job and how God allowed the devil to test him because he knew Job would go through the storm. Job may have doubted God a little, but he remained faithful to God and because of that, Job received double blessings. As I sat there, I wondered if I was being tested or was I being semi-mental. I understood from the message about Mephibosheth that he was crippled by the hands of someone else, but there was still room for him at the king's table. When I heard that, I felt a warm sensation come over me. It was like the angel and devil had come back to sit on my shoulders, but this time it was different. When the altar call was made, I could not sit there. I did not pay any attention to that little voice that was saying don't get up. All I could hear was, get up and make that step.

I took one deep breath, got up, went down front and sat in the chair. As I heard the congregation saying "amen" and clapping, in my heart, it seemed like something was being lifted off me. While sitting in the chair, I heard a voice say, "I got you." It was the sweetest voice I had ever heard. I felt comforted like never before. I opened my tear-filled eyes and felt the touch of my oldest daughter. She was standing by my side crying harder than I was. Then here comes my baby girl, also with tears in her eyes and she sat on my lap. It hit me that I had to get myself together for my daughters. When the Pastor asked me if I had anything to say, I could not speak. My tears spoke for me. That day I joined the church. More importantly, I surrendered to God. I realized I had to learn to trust someone, and God was all I had left. I had always been the type to say, 'if I am going to do something, I was going to do it right.' So, I attended Bible study, Sunday school and church services. There was a burning inside me that I just could not explain. I continued to attend church, read my Bible, and ask questions. Let me tell you that the struggle was real. It seemed like everything that could come my way, came hard.

Chapter 7

When you make it up in your mind to do the right thing, that is when all hell breaks loose. When people heard I was going to church, they tried to hinder me. They attacked my character, talked about my mom and said things that they thought they knew. One person even said I was dating the Pastor which was far from the truth and this was coming from family. Mom was in a nursing home at this time. When I told her I was back in church and trying to get my life together, she was upset that I did not return to my old church. By this time, Agape had a new pastor and most of the members had moved on to other churches or died. There was a lot of hurt for me at my old church. The old church was where I found

85

out about all the lies surrounding my life. My dad who was an usher at the church had molested me for years so I just could not stay there. I don't think Mom took me seriously at all. When I told my best friend, Aunt Dee, and my sister, they were happy and thrilled for me.

Aunt Dee said, "God had something special for me and although people may count me out, God has the final say."

As far back as I can remember, my Aunt Dee was that special person in my life. Even though she had a family of her own, she always managed to make me smile with kind words or just being there for me. I was determined to stay on the battlefield. Lifeway Church was a blessing to me. They accepted my children and me in the congregation. I even noticed how my girls became happier and they enjoyed going to Lifeway also. As the years went by, I learned that there was a process to being healed. Healing does not come automatically. The first thing I had to do was get in touch with the pain. I had to bring my pain to the surface. It had been buried inside me for so long I was not really in touch with my feelings. I was more in touch with the hurt and anger that comes with pain. My pain was so far from my conscious mind that it took a long time for me to connect with my real feelings. Years of hurt, feelings of abandonment, and lies were buried underneath depression, sadness, madness, and a "get them before they get you" attitude. I knew I had to get rid of all that mess. Some people try to cope with their problems through drugs and alcohol and some go to therapy for help. I am not saying there is anything wrong with going to therapy, but at the time, it was not for me. I had to get into my Bible and pray to God continuously. I learned that God is love and I wanted to know everything about that love. So, I wrote on white recipe cards, 90 scriptures from the Bible about love. I learned a verse each week. I took the card to work, repeated it until it was in my spirit. I patterned it after what David said in Psalms 119:11 "Thy word have I laid up in my heart, that I might not sin against thee." That scripture was one of the first verses I learned in Sunday school at Agape Baptist Church. I did not understand it then, but I sure understand it now. I wanted the love of God and the only way I knew I could get it was through His word. After I learned those scriptures, my heart was changing. I cried a lot. Nobody had done anything to me, but I just cried when I felt like it. Then God let me know that this was the second part of the process of healing. At that moment, there was a breakthrough. The barrier between my mind and my spirit was broken. My spirit took over. God worked on my behalf and started to change things in my life. I was in control of my emotions and I wasn't in control of what happened to me. I cried when I wanted to and never let anyone see me cry. I was brought up with the idea of "never let them see you sweat." This means, I never showed my emotions and always tried to be in control. The moment I started learning the love scriptures, I lost control and God took control. It is all a part of the process. We must give up control and that is what I did not want to do. But God is stronger than you or me. He could have just taken control of me, but He wanted me to relinquish control. Your greatest blessing will come when you give God control. I learned through this second phase of healing that tears cleanse you. It seemed like the more I cried, the better I was feeling. I did not like it when people saw me emotional or crying, but during this time of my life, I did not care. Through my tears, God was cleaning me from the inside. Through my tears, I was releasing my hurts, pains, and the feeling of abandonment. I was beginning to let go of anger and animosity. I started to experience what some would call the emotional stutter. I wanted to stop this process in my mind because it was a painful process. I had a resistance and there was mental activity going on to try to stop this process. In my mind, I battled with feeling of stupidity for going through the process and thinking it would never work or that I was not good enough for God to use me. The more this message played in my mind or in my heart, I knew I had to keep moving forward. One thing about the mind is that it stores all your hurt and pain. The mind will tell you "that's enough and stop doing this to yourself." It is true that your mind is the devil's workshop until you get the mind of Christ. As I was going through, I kept meditating on Philippians 2:5, "Have this mind in you which was also in Christ Jesus."

I had to keep my mind on the love scriptures and Philippians 2:5. I wanted the mind of Christ because the mind that I had at the moment was doing me more harm than good. I had to heal from past hurts and wounds. I needed to be right for my girls. I needed more for me. I wanted to feel the God that everyone was talking about. I wanted to hear His voice. I learned through the word of God, that sometimes you must be quiet and listen for God's voice. I spent so many years being hurt and angry that I did not know what God's voice sounded like. In this cleansing process, I learned that God speaks to your heart and not your mind. The next phase of the healing process for me was evaluation. Determine in your heart that what you have just been cleansed from is gone forever. You have to adjust your lifestyle to the changes that you're asking God to do in your life. God will put love, peace, and joy in the places where He has cleansed you.

I had to re-think and re-evaluate my perception and how I looked at things. I did not believe in God when I was younger because I did not think He loved me or even knew who I was. I began to see God in a new light; I began to feel His love. I was seeing past my pains and hurts. I was no longer looking at what was done to me. I was looking at setting myself free from the jail of hatred. I began seeing myself as somebody and a peculiar person. I am somebody. I don't have to be what everyone says that I am. You see, I had been told in my life that I would never be nothing because my mother was nothing, my dad was nothing, and nothing from nothing leaves nothing. That's why we should watch what we say to our children. Negative words breed negative results. If you talk negative to a child, he/she will be negative, and their actions will be negative. I was learning I did not have to be who they said my mother and father were. I called this my "aha moment." I was feeling God, I was hearing God, and I was feeling His love. Now, I am not saying I am completely healed, but I am releasing my pains and hurts. This is an ongoing process. I still have issues that I am trying to heal from, but one of the things I know about this process is that it always has a positive effect. While you are being healed by God, your healing will be in vain if you don't forgive the people/person who hurt you. I was being healed, but to complete the process meant I had to learn how to forgive.

I think that was the hardest thing for me to do. So once again, I went to the Bible and looked up all the scriptures on forgiveness. I found 20 powerful verses on forgiveness. Forgiveness is a powerful tool and really sets you free. It is true forgiveness is "for you" and helps you to free yourself. I had been holding on to grudges for years. It seems like I had a grudge against everyone from my biological mother to my adopted mom, both dads, the two men that raped me, and just people in general. If anyone had done anything to me in the past, I wanted to get revenge.

When I started to mediate on forgiveness scriptures, it changed my attitude.

First, I meditated on Colossians 3:13, "Make allowance for each other's faults and forgive anyone who offends you. Remember, the Lord forgave you, so you must forgive others."

When I was in Bible college, I read about Buddha and one thing that stuck in my mind is that he said, "Holding on to anger is like grasping a hot coal with the intent of throwing it at someone else; you are the one that gets burned."

I share that to say, all those years I was holding on to grudges and having built up anger that did nothing but burn me and cause me to lose out on so much of life. Now I was no longer going to let that anger keep me from losing out on life, my children, and what God has to offer me. I learned that to forgive I had to let go of my anger and negative thoughts. I had to forgive people deep within myself as well as outward. Forgiveness is not just a formality, but a state of mind. That loving, accepting state of mind can lift you from burdens both mentally and physically. One thing about it, true forgiveness is easier said than done. It is hard to forgive someone who has constantly hurt you in a way that contradicts your values and morals. I had years of unforgiveness in my heart, and it did not fix a thing. To be healed I had to let go of the coal. How could I forgive my mom for lying to me all these years? How could I forgive my dad for molesting me or Janice and my father for abandoning me? What about the people who raped me? How could I forgive them? I really did not know if I wanted to forgive people, but through prayer, I realized that if I wanted to move forward I had to embrace forgiveness. I was not hurting anyone but myself by not forgiving. I realized that hurt would always remain as a part of my life, but forgiveness can lessen its grip on me and help me focus on the positive things in my life. I have learned to forgive. Not forgiving people was allowing me to be a victim. I had to realize that because Jesus died for me, it made me victorious, and I did not have to be a victim of the past. I had to move on. God has so much for me to do. I cannot be the mother that God ordained me to be while being a victim. I had the love of God in me, so I was not a victim. I was determined to walk in the newness of God. When I held onto unforgiveness, I gave power to the ones who violated me. Now it was time for me to take back my God-given power.

So, I made up in my mind to forgive everyone who hurt me, lied to me or abused me.

Chapter 8

I went to the nursing home to visit my Mom. As I sat by her bedside, I looked at her and said, "Mom I forgive you." I just had to forgive people in my heart. Today, I can truly say I forgive all the people who have hurt me. I am free from the feeling of abandonment. I forgive my real mother for not raising me. I forgive all the people who made fun of me and said I would never amount to anything. I forgive the ones who stole my innocence. I had to ask God to forgive me for not believing or trusting in Him. The biggest thing was I had to forgive myself. I think that was the hardest thing to do. Forgiving yourself is essential. We tend to hold ourselves more accountable than we do others. Forgiving yourself is not really addressed in the Bible, but there are principles regarding forgiveness that we can apply to forgiving ourselves. When God forgives us, He no longer remembers our sins. (Jeremiah 31:34) This does not mean God forgets, but because He forgives us and chooses not to bring up our sins in a negative way. Peter states in Acts 10:34, "In truth I perceive that God shows no partiality." No partiality on the matter of forgiveness is that God does not choose to forgive one person and not another. I feel it is just as important to forgive ourselves as it is for us to forgive others. Forgiving yourself is simply letting go of what you are holding against you, so you can move on with God. Proverbs 16:25 states, "There is a way that seems right to a man, but its end is the way of death." The energy we take to harbor anger, hatred, and resentment is exhaustive. Every bit of energy we give to negative activities and dwelling on regrets robs us of the energy we need to become the person God wants us to be. It is vital to forgive yourself.

Letting go of hurt, pain, and learning to forgive people and myself, has helped me to become whole in God. I can move forward and leave my past behind. I am not yet healed from everything that happened in my life, but day by day, I become more victorious. I can move forward in life and provide for my girls. I now can give them the love that was robbed from me. I can love unconditional since I let Jesus in my life, and He brought a new meaning to life. I now can handle disappointments. I know that battles are not mine they are the Lord's. I am not saying that just because I am healed everything is great. I would be lying to you and to myself. I still have flashbacks sometimes, but during those times, I get my Bible and talk to God.

After being committed to the church for a few years and trying to learn all that I could about God, I started to move more into a worship mode. I would praise God for helping me to get over some of the things that happened in my life. Worshiping God was a different experience for me. Worship is the feeling or expression of reverence and adoration for God. I really did not know I was worshipping God I just thought I was praising God.

One Sunday, a lady said to me "Girl you really worshiped God today. He is working on you. God is getting ready to use you in a mighty way. You just wait and see."

I really did not understand worship. I just knew it went with praise and it was the same thing. One day at Bible study, I asked the question what the difference between praise and worship. I felt kind on dumb because I thought I should have already known the answer. The Pastor explained it, but I had to get a deeper interpretation of praise and worship. So once again, I went to the Bible and looked up everything I could on praise and worship. I found out that praise is about God, and what He does for us; however, worship is to God. Praise is opening up, and worship is entering in. I have come to the conclusion, that praise is boldly declaring, and worship is humbly bowing in the presence of a Holy God. Praise applauds what God has done, but worship is honoring God for who He is. I could not believe it. The person who felt like God did not love her, the person who was not sure there was a God, is now humbling herself and bowing down to God. It seemed like the more I praised and worshipped God the closer I was drawn to him. I was beginning to believe I did have a purpose.

It seemed like God was calling me to do something, but I did not know what. I had only been serious about God for a few years. I thought it was to be an usher or sing in the choir. I tried those things, but I felt there was something more. I talked to a friend one day about it and she suggested I should talk to the pastor. I was skeptical about talking to him because I still did not trust men. I told her I would, but I could not put myself up to calling him. One day I was just going through, it seemed like my heart was heavy. I could not relax or sleep. I decided to call my Aunt and a man answered her phone. I thought this is not my uncle, so I hung up. I redialed the number feeling certain I was dialing my Aunt and a man answers again. I asked who he was, and he replied Pastor Johnson. I apologized and told him I was trying to call my Aunt. He said, "no you dialed the right number."

Now I knew I was not stupid and had dialed my Aunt's number. Then he said he had been waiting for my call and asked if I could meet him at the church soon. Reluctantly I said yes. I called the lady who was hosting Bible study at her house and asked if she would go with me. She agreed, and we met the pastor at the church. We prayed first then he asked me what was going on. I told him I thought it was a medical problem and I don't think he could help me. I said I was calling my Aunt to talk to her about it and I don't know how I dialed your number.

He had a slight smile on his face and said, "You didn't dial me God did. He knew you needed to talk to me, not your Aunt. I really did not know what God was doing so I just went with the flow."

I thought to myself, I am trying to do a new thing in Christ and I need to accept anything God is doing. I began telling the pastor how I was feeling.

I said, "I can't sleep, sometimes I feel like I am having a heart attack. I just don't feel right. I guess I need to go to the doctor."

He looked at Rhonda and I and said, "You don't need a doctor you need to surrender."

I said, "Surrender, I thought that's what I was doing. Now I am confused. I had been going to this church for about three years. I have learned and studied God's word. I opened myself up to accept Jesus as my Lord and Savior. I am praying, I am praising; I am worshipping God. I am learning how to let go and forgive. I am not angry like I used to be. I have changed my lifestyle and my children are happy. Wow, I am happier than

I've been in a long time. So, what more does God want from me? I went from not liking You to loving You. God, what more do you want from me?"

Pastor Johnson looked at me and said, "God has a job for you." Obviously, I looked puzzled because he said, "I can't tell you what it is."

I thought, what! This is just a waste of my time and I was beginning to get a little upset with Pastor Johnson.

I said, "Why can't you tell me? You are the pastor. Right?"

He replied, "I can't tell you, God has to tell you."

Then he asked me if I had ever been on a fast? I told him I had been on one before but did not complete it. Pastor Johnson told me to go on a weekend fast, and I was to eat fruits and vegetables only along with water. The fast was to start Thursday at midnight and end at midnight on Saturday. I thought that is a lot, but I could do it. My friend, Rhonda, offered to go on it with me.

The Pastor said, "No this is something she is going to have to do by herself." Pastor Johnson said that after completing the fast and before church time Sunday morning, I would have my answer. He also told me to pray before I start and not to let anyone else know that I was on a fast. I agreed and then left. I only had a few hours before I started the fast. I knew it was going to be hard for me to go without food, but I still had to cook for my kids. I went to the store and bought different fruits and vegetables, and some I did not even like. But, hey, in my heart I really wanted to do it.

That night as I put my girls to bed, I kept looking at my clock. It seemed like it took forever for midnight to come. Finally, the clock struck 12 and I knelt and prayed.

I prayed, "God I have never been on this kind of fast. I need your help, and I need to know what You want me to do. I had no problem with the fast on Friday, even the girls were on board until we passed a McDonalds. But I did not hold them to the fast. The crazy thing about it was that they ate McDonald's and my fruit. Saturday was kind of hard, but I was determined to stay on my fast. The children and I were invited to a barbecue at a local park. I did not want to go, but my girls had been looking forward to going all week long. So, I took my water and went to the barbecue. As soon as I got there, all I could see was food. My brother was grilling ribs, hamburger, chicken, and hotdogs. There was potatoes salad, chips, pop, baked beans, macaroni and cheese, cakes, and pies on the table. I think they had every kind of food one could think of, and I was like God You have to help me, please. At least they did have a vegetable I could eat and some fruit. I really did enjoy myself at the cookout; however, everyone was wondered why I didn't eat any of the other dishes. I never told them the real reason. I think I just said I was not hungry. We stayed at the park for about five hours. When we left, my brother insisted that I take a plate home. I piled it up with food. I planned to really eat after midnight. I got home and settled in with the girls as on the couches down stairs. Around 11:30, I fixed a plate of food and put it in the microwave. I thought to myself, when it is one minute after midnight, I was going to heat up my plate and eat. I joined my oldest daughter on the couch, while my baby girl slept on the loveseat. I was watching a movie and I dozed off. I don't know how long I was sleep, but the next thing I know I felt shaking on me. I heard a man's voice. I woke up, but I could not see anyone. I thought I was dreaming, but I could not move. I was in a trance. I laid there, and this voice said, "I have something for you to do."

The voice was clear, but it was not a loud voice.

I said, "Huh?"

He said it again. I could not speak, and I could not move.

Then the voice said, "I want you to proclaim the gospel."

I remember thinking to proclaim the gospel.

Then the voice said, "I have ordained you to go and proclaim the good news. I am calling you for a greater work. I am calling you to go and proclaim the gospel."

Then just as the voice came, it left. Now, I know it was the voice of God. I tell you I was scared to move for a minute. I got up and looked at my girls to make sure they were ok. I don't know if I was scared or still in a daze. I thought someone was in my house. I checked my locks. I looked in my kitchen and went to see if anyone was there. I did not want to wake the girls, so I eased upstairs and checked all the rooms. No one was there, no one had come in, and I really did not know what to do. I wanted to call Rhonda and Dee and tell them what had happened, but it was three o'clock in the morning. I could not wake them up. I also could not believe what just happened to me. I could not go back to sleep for a while. I kept thinking proclaim the Gospel? I finally went to sleep for a few hours. It was time to get ready for church and I still had mixed emotions about what happened. Did I hear the voice of God, or was I just dreaming? Am I imagining things or was I still in a slight daze?

Chapter 9

As we were getting ready for church, my oldest daughter kept asking me if something was wrong with me. I asked her if she heard someone in the house that night. Of course, she said no. I knew my baby girl was a light sleeper, so I asked her the same thing and she said no. Naturally, they were confused but I just played it off, we all got dressed and went to church. I was a little scared to go in because I did not know what was going to happen. When I got inside the church, the first person I saw was the Pastor. He asked me to come to his office and requested Rhonda to come also.

When we were all in the office, he just simply asked, "Do you have something to tell me."

I cleared my throat and said, "Well, I think so."

I explained to him what happened and how strong but sweet and calming the voice was. I told him I heard that I was to proclaim the gospel. Rhonda looked at me, started smiling and Pastor said, "Do you know what that means?"

I said I think I am supposed to preach. Then Pastor asked if I had gotten a confirmation scripture. The next thing I knew, Luke 4:18 came out of my mouth. Pastor looked at me and said, "Now you know what God wants you to do. Now you have to do it."

He told me we would talk again later, but I really did not connect the scripture I blurted out with our conversation. I opened up my Bible and looked up the scripture. I could not believe what it read.

Luke 4:18 says, "The spirit of the Lord is upon me, because he has anointed me to preach the gospel to the poor, he hath sent me to heal the brokenhearted, to preach deliverance to the captives, and recovering of sight to the blind, to set at liberty them that are bruised."

That was a WOW moment for me. I had been brokenhearted, needed deliverance from a few more things, had been so blind about the things of God, and now God wanted me to go and preach.

All of it was very hard for me because I came from a church that did not believe in women preachers. Was this a joke? I didn't know if I believed in women preachers, yet this was my assignment from God. How could I do this? What was I going to do? I left church confused and decided talk to Aunt Dee. I told her the whole story about the voice in the middle of the night. What the pastor said my confirmation scripture. I told her I know how people feel about women preachers. As usual, she gave me words of wisdom and she said, "You have to do what God is telling you to do. Don't worry about people. If this is your assignment, accept it and let God use you. I believe in you, and I am proud of you."

I knew right then that I had to proclaim the gospel because God had chosen me. Now the big problem was going to the nursing home and telling my mom. She has never believed in women preachers, so this was going to be interesting. That following Sunday I had another talk with my pastor and told him I was accepting the call to the ministry. However, I needed to tell my family before I announced it to the congregation.

I went to the nursing home to tell my mom, and it went just as I expected. She told me I was being brainwashed by my pastor. Women were not supposed to preach and I was going to hell. I walked away from her feeling down, but I was determined to do what God had called me to do. I had a serious conversation with my daughters and told them what I was going to do. At first, I had some resistance from my oldest daughter; she did not want to be a preacher's kid. I don't think that my youngest daughter cared one way or the other.

Then I went to talk to my sister, who was raised in a church with a woman pastor. I got such comfort from her. She told me I had to do what God called me to do and no matter what she would stand by my side. I must say to this day that my sister has done just what she said she would do. Every time I have preached she was there supporting me. She even would sing for me before I preach. She has been a great support system. It was crazy because I had mixed feelings about being called to the ministry. I still did not think I heard from God correctly. He wanted me to preach, and I thought I couldn't do it. I didn't know enough to preach and didn't think anyone would listen to me. I thought I was nobody, and no one would take me seriously. All those things ran through my mind, but then I had to think and reflect to the scriptures. God is awesome. When you need a scripture, He will guide you to the right one at the right time, or through someone else. I told Rhonda and her husband, my feelings about the call to the ministry. They led me to a scripture that covered everything I had been feeling. Jeremiah received a call from the Lord, and he was afraid of speaking because he was so young. But God told him that He ordained him before he was born, and he had a job to do. God spoke to Jeremiah and told him not to be afraid of their faces (Jeremiah 1:5-8). When I read those words, it seemed like God was talking to me. I knew that I had a job to do, and if I was going to be all I could in God, I could not be afraid of their faces. Just like Jeremiah, God ordained me before he formed me in my mother's belly. No matter what people thought, I had to do it, but God knew I was scared.

I was lying in bed one night still thinking about proclaiming the gospel, and a scripture kept coming in my mind. I kept hearing Romans 8:30 so I finally got my Bible and started reading. I thought ok God, I got the message, that passage gave me more confirmation. "And whom he foreordained, them he also called: and whom he called, them he also justified; and whom he justified, them he also glorified. What then shall we say to these things? If God is for us, who can be against us."

Then I knew that when I openly accept the call of God, it will not matter what people think as long as God is for me, He's more than the world against me. That following Sunday I was supposed to let the congregation know that I had been called to the ministry. I don't know what happened, but I just could not get up to do it. The Pastor knew I was supposed to let the congregation know, so there was a time in the service, he asked if anyone had anything to say. I looked away, but I could feel him staring at me. I just sat there. I could not get up and say anything. Although I felt kind of bad, I just could not do it. When I got home from church, the pastor called me and asked what happened and why didn't I make my announcement? I told him I wanted him to do it for me, but he said I had to do it. I was disappointed in myself, and I felt like I had let God down. God had brought me so far, and

125

I couldn't do that one thing. I prayed and prayed to God. I just wanted to make sure I was doing the right thing. One night I was reading my Bible in bed and fell asleep with it on my chest. What happened next was like part of the story in the Christmas Carol when the spirits came to visit Scrooge. Once again, I felt the touch of someone, I could not see the face, but perhaps he was an angel and he told to go with him. The next thing I know I was standing on a rock and I saw a whole lot of people who were arguing. I recognized the man they were hollering at, it was Moses.

I said, "What's going on?" to the angel.

He said, "Everybody is not going to listen to you, some people are going to rise up against you." Then we left. The next place we went to was

Jesse's house, but we were in a field, and from far away I saw a little dirty boy carrying a staff.

I said, "Is that David."

He said, "Yes, he is dirty, he stinks, he feels left out and rejected by his family." I thought my life situations had left me feeling dirty, I had stinking thinking, and I felt left out and rejected by many, but God choose him to be king, then suddenly, we left. Next, we went to the potter's house, and as we were standing there I saw a man sitting down at a pottery wheel. As he worked with the clay, he would look at it and reworked it again. We stood there for a few minutes, but nothing was said then the angel said, "Let's go."

As we were leaving, I looked back at the man and the pottery and I saw my face in the clay.

I said that's my face on there, and he said, "yes, God wants to make you and mold you. All you have to do is put yourself in His hands."

Then we left from there, and the next thing I recall is we were on a balcony. There were so many people below us I could not count them. They were yelling, screaming, and pointing at me as if they were mad at me.

I said, "who are they?"

The angel said, "Oh they are on their way to hell."

I said, "Well why are they mad at me? Why are they pointing and screaming at me?"

Then the angel said something that changed me forever, he said, "Because you knew the word that could save them, and you did not tell them."

Those words were like a stab in my heart. The angel left and I was on this balcony looking and listening to the people pointing and hollering at me.

After that, I woke up in a sweat with the Bible still on my chest. I resolved in my mind that I was going to preach and proclaim the gospel. I could hardly wait until Sunday to publically announce my calling to the ministry. That Sunday, when the pastor said, does anyone have anything to say, I quickly jumped up. I told the congregation that I was accepting the call to the ministry. Some of them were accepting and happy for me, but a lot of them were not. I could not let that stop me. Life has not been easy being a woman in ministry, but God has always made a way. There were a lot of people who doubted my call. One person even called the church and told my pastor he needed to watch me because I was a manipulator and there was no way God would have called me. I was met with a lot of opposition concerning the ministry, especially from my family. One great thing I had was a strong church family who kept me motivated in doing what God called me to do. My sister, Aunt Dee, and my best friend, Kate, were always there for me. Soon after I entered the ministry, my mom died. No matter what I went through as a child or what she did or did not do she raised me and I loved her. When she died, it broke my heart. One thing about her death, I learned how people really felt about me. Some relationships were not as strong as I thought they were. I felt that after

Mom died, a lot her family did not treat me the same way. Now I did not say all of them, but a lot of them treated me as though I did not matter since her death. They catered more to my brother than me, but that was ok because my church family was there for me. A year later, my dad passed but I did not feel hurt. I tried to play the role like I was upset, but it just did not work. When I looked at him in the casket, I just thought that was what he got for what he did to me. I felt bad because my girls asked me why I did not cry at his funeral like I did at Mom's funeral. I just told them I was all cried out, but deep in my heart, I wished he had died before my mom. I know that was bad for me to say but it was the truth at the time. God is still working on me. Today I can say that I have honestly forgiven my dad for what he did. One thing I have learned is that I can't change the past. I can't predict tomorrow, so the only thing I can do is live from day to day. I am not going to hold onto unforgiveness. Of the two people that raped me, one is dead and the other one is still alive. I forgive them both. I have learned to open my heart and trust people, and through this experience I have gained so many meaningful relationships.

Now I am not saying that it was easy, but little by little, I have slowly let the walls come down. I used to keep people far away and I would only let them know so much about me. I did not want to get close to anyone on a personal level. The more I got God in my heart, the more the walls of seclusion came down. So, no matter what people say, I have learned that what God has for me is for me.

I still have a long way to go to be who God has called me to be. Just like the late James Cleveland wrote, "I don't believe he brought me this far to leave me," and I feel the same way. As I entered the ministry, my life changed so much. I never thought I would be able to stand in front of people and proclaim the gospel. I never thought I would leave the little town, my home, where I was born and raised. I figured I would raise my children there and be buried there. But God had other plans. When I was in Indiana, I had a good job, started going to Bible College. I was able to buy a home, which was something I always wanted. When the opportunity came, and I jumped right on it. Soon after buying the home, the Lord spoke to me and said I was going to move. I thought, 'no Lord I just bought this house.' God spoke to me and said, "I didn't tell you to buy it."

At the time, I had met a woman Pastor and we became friends. She lived in Kentucky, so I was traveling to Kentucky a lot to preach. She had just started a church and I had just graduated from Bible College. She needed help and since it was not far from Indiana, I would go there every two weeks and help her at the church. I also started receiving and accepting preaching engagements. One day, I was sitting on her porch about to travel home with my girls. She said that the Lord told her I was going to move to Kentucky. I thought, no

He did not tell you that, especially when I just bought a house.

I just smiled and said, "ok," and left it at that.

As I was driving home from Indiana, the Lord spoke to me and said, "You see all the leaves on those trees, they represent your blessings. If you do what I tell you to do, I have plans for you. If you just trust me, you will be blessed."

I thought about it and when I got home, I asked the girls what they thought about moving to Kentucky. My youngest daughter just said whatever you want Mom. My oldest daughter was determined she was not going to Kentucky. I understood that because she was in high school and was a great basketball player. All her friends and family were in Indiana and I was trying to take that away from her. I thought maybe I am being selfish, but God kept telling me I needed to move to Kentucky for my blessings. Then I had others telling me I was being overzealous in the ministry and I was not experienced enough to move. Also, maybe I was just moving so I would be accepted. This went on for about a month. I was still traveling back and forth to Kentucky. God kept telling me He was going to bless me there. I was beginning to lose sleep again because all I could think about was that I just got the house, it was my dream home. I had a good job and my daughter did not want to leave. Then I thought, well I could leave her with my family, but I did not want to split up my family. So, after one trip to Kentucky,

I was so confused, I decided to stay home from work. That day I thought God it has to be just me and You. After the girls went to school, I got my Bible and started asking God questions. I asked God why I had to leave my home. Why are You telling me to leave? How can I hurt my children like this? What are You doing to me, God?

That night, my sister called me, and she said I was on her mind all day. My sister and I talked all the time, but the crazy thing was that she answered every question I asked God earlier that day. She told me God had a plan for me that was bigger than where I was. She said God was molding me for something great, and for me to get the benefit of it I needed to move out of my town. Now the strange thing about this is that I did not tell her I was thinking about moving. She also said God wanted to keep my family together. If the kids had a problem with it, I was the adult and everywhere I go I needed to continue to take my kids with me. After I got off the phone with my sister, I was in awe. Through her, God gave me some answers. But still, there was my oldest daughter who did not want to leave. I knew she could stay with my sister or my niece, but I did not want to leave her. I could not really protect her from a different city. I needed her to be with me, but I did not want to force her to go. I knew if I did, our relationship would not be a good one. So, I prayed to God, and told Him if this was His will for me to leave and move to Kentucky, would He please make it all right with my daughter to come with me. I told God I did not want to break up my family, but it had to be right in her heart. I prayed that prayer on a Tuesday and that Friday night I was lying in my room, and the girls were in their room. I heard them talking, but I really did not pay attention to their conversation. A few minutes later, both came in my room and lay across my bed, which they did often. My oldest daughter began to cry, and she said she really didn't want to move. If God told me to move and I had to go there so I could preach, she would go with me. By this time, we all were crying she said she didn't want to live without her sister and me. God had answered all my questions.

Chapter 10

I sold my home and moved to Kentucky. I wish I could tell you that when I moved life was a bed of roses because it was not. I did meet some amazing friends, and we are still friends today. However, when I say the struggle was real, it was real! Many times, I wanted to move back home. I kept replaying that vision God showed me on the highway about my blessings. I kept hearing my sister's voice confirming what God said as He spoke through her. I did not want to seem like a failure to my kids, so I stuck through it, prayed a lot, and endured a lot. As I looked back on it today, it all was a learning experience. Through my move to Kentucky, I have seen the good and the bad of ministry. I have learned how to treat people and how not to treat people. Ministry has opened so many doors for my children and me. When I first started in the ministry, I was an introvert. I never liked to speak in public. I had to really meditate on 2 Timothy 1:7 "For God hath not given us the spirit of fear; but of power, and love, and of a sound mind."

When I got that in my spirit, I received holy boldness from God. I always had the power, but I just had to activate it. I learned that everything I went through was all in God's plan. I realized it was a process for me to reach a point where I totally trusted God.

Through this great call of God, I have traveled to many places teaching, preaching, and even singing the gospel. I have truly learned the meaning of Philippians 4:13, "I can do all things through Christ which strengthens me."

When I say that I mean I can do all things, through my trials, Christ helps me to endure through tough times. He also helps me to grow during those times. I see my faith grow right in the face of my battles. God will equip you with the armor you need to stand firm. So, when you go through trials, remember you too can do all things through Christ Jesus.

When you realize that, you will be able to "Count it all joy when you face trials of many kinds, because the testing of your faith produces perseverance, let perseverance finish its work so that you may be mature and complete, not lacking anything" (paraphrasing James 1:2-4).

143

Now I have learned contentment through Jesus Christ. If there is a fight that we go through, it is a constant struggle to be content. Disappointments, setbacks, and delays sometimes beat us down. We will easily become bitter and entitled because the world tells us we deserve to be happy, and it is easy for us to slip into that mindset. But through Christ, we take our focus off the things we don't have, the frustrations that surround us, and we put the focus on where it needs to be which is serving God.

Paul explains this better in Philippians 4:12, "I know what it is to be in need, and I know what it is to have plenty. I have learned the secret of being content in any and every situation, whether well fed or hungry, whether living in plenty or in want."

This type of contentment can only come from God. I have also gained strength through the victory of Jesus Christ. When we understand that Jesus died on our behalf and rose as a true conqueror. We will understand that what He accomplished was credited to our account and we were set free. Justice demanded that I should die, but God has already paid the price.

That is why John 16:33 states, "I have told you these things, in me you may have peace, in this world you will have trouble. But take heart! I have overcome the world."

For too long I have missed what I needed looking for what I wanted. Now I have found true joy, true happiness, and a true meaning of life. I love my biological mother so much today. We are very close and I must say. she is a remarkable woman who has overcome many obstacles herself. I thank God that she is in my life today.

As I look back on my life, I now see how God was working behind the scenes of my life. There was a time when I did not even know if I believed in God.   Consuming my life with bitterness, hurt, and anger only took away from my life. Now my life is consumed with love, peace, and joy. I have learned not to look at people and wonder when they are going to hurt me. Now I look at people and wonder how I can bless them. I am so proud of who I am today. I don't worry about my looks anymore. I am comfortable with who I am today. My hair can be short or long. My weight may go up and down, but as long as my heart belongs to God, the rest does not matter. I have learned to love myself and treat myself right. I don't need anyone to pamper me because I am going to pamper myself. I used to think I did not deserve anything. Now, I know that I am a child of God and I deserve the best of everything God has for me. By learning to love myself, I have learned to love others. I am talking about that agape love. In loving others, you must see people how God sees them. You must learn to forgive people. Life is too short. God is too good for us to walk around in sadness and bitterness.

As I look back on my life, I urge parents to talk more to their children and look for behavior changes in your child. God entrusted that child to you. Love your child and hug your child. One of my friends always says, "A child should have at least 20 hugs a day from their parents."

One thing that I can say is my mother did not send me to church, we went to church together. It is true what the scripture says, "Train up a child in the way he should go; and when he is old, he will not depart from it."

I was trained up in church, even when I thought I was not paying attention. When I called myself mad at God, there was a seed planted in me. Through abuse and all the things that I went through, that seed was still there. I may not have watered it, but somebody was praying for me. Train your child up because when they are old, I am a living witness, they will not depart.

For those who were abused and felt like giving up, everyone else may have counted you out, but God has counted you in. Just trust in God and know that you are special. God has a plan for your life. Makes no different what you have been through or who hurt you in the past, just remember you have a friend in Jesus. God will take your burdens and turn them into blessings. He will turn hurt into happiness, pain into peace, and hate into love. I am a living witness to what God can do. He took my old hard heart and filled it with His love. I thank God for His grace and mercy. From my mother's womb, He knew me and through heartaches and pain, He groomed me. Through all my test and trials, God gave me a testimony. I am not where I used to be, not where I want to be, but striving to get to where God needs me to be. There is a story behind my praise. Trust God and trust the plan that he has for your life. God has brought me from the Pit of my life, to the pulpit to preach his word, and for that I say Thank you God!!!!

www.ingramcontent.com/pod-product-compliance
Lightning Source LLC
Chambersburg PA
CBHW051840090426
42736CB00011B/1902